© 1990 Franklin Watts

First published in Great Britain in 1990 by
Franklin Watts
96 Leonard Street
London EC2A 4RH

First published in Australia by
Franklin Watts
14 Mars Road
Lane Cove
NSW 2066

UK ISBN: 0 7496 0153 1

Printed in Belgium

This book is printed on recycled paper. The
Publishers regret any consequent lack of quality of
reproduction of the photographs and illustrations.

Editor
Ruth Taylor

Picture researcher
Sarah Ridley

Designed by
Sally Boothroyd

Illustrations by
Tony Kenyon
Raymond Turvey
Matthew White

Photographs
Courtesy of Alcan Aluminium Can Recycling page
17(B); Dennis Barnes 23(L); courtesy of British Steel
Tinplate 19, 28; Ecoscene 8, 10, 20, 27; Eye
Ubiquitous 13(T), 13(B), 18; Chris Fairclough Colour
Library 16; Hutchison Library 23(R); courtesy of
International Tin Research Institute 15, 21; Maggie
Murray/Format 9; Brenda Prince/Format 6-7;
courtesy of Reynolds Aluminum 17(T); ZEFA 11.

A CIP catalogue record for this book is
available from the British Library.

Recycling
METAL

Joy Palmer

Franklin Watts

London/New York/Sydney/Toronto

CONTENTS

Throughout the world, metal is collected for recycling. This heap of tins has been sorted at a rubbish tip at Smokey Mountain in the Philippines.

INTRODUCTION

The word *waste* means something that is left over after use, superfluous and no longer serving a purpose. For a long time people have been in the habit of throwing away such materials, believing that they no longer have value. Indeed, we live in a throwaway society and it can be all too easy to discard leftovers into a bin to be collected and disposed of. Most wastes, however, are far too valuable to throw away. Metal waste, whether from household or industry, certainly falls into this category.

Metal is one of the four main ingredients of domestic waste, the others being organic matter (such as food scraps), paper and glass. In total, metals make up around 9 per cent by weight of household leftovers.

There are various ways to deal with waste: for example, it may be buried in the ground or burned. Whatever we do with waste, it cannot just disappear from the world as if by magic. Buried waste may be out of sight — but it is a potential source of problems, for example, the leaking of poisonous substances into the soil. The incineration of waste may also be problematic — perhaps gas and smoke will be released to pollute the air we breathe. Without doubt, waste must be controlled and managed efficiently. The best possible solution is to recycle waste, that is, to claim it back again and re-use it, perhaps in a different form.

The topic of metals is vast; so the limited space available here is used to concentrate on those metals most commonly found in our own waste, namely iron/steel, aluminium and tin.

METALS TO WASTE?

Waste metal comes from both household and industrial sources. In Britain and the United States, by weight, metals account for around 9 per cent of the total domestic waste. An inspection of the "average" family dustbin will no doubt reveal a vast assortment of cans that once contained items ranging from beer to beans and soup to sausages. Over eleven thousand million metal food and drink cans are purchased in Britain every year. Taking the national average, each person uses one can every day.

Such amazingly high figures illustrate what a remarkable amount of aluminium, tin and steel is regularly tossed into the waste disposal stream of the nation. Yet far from being superfluous junk, these cans can be reclaimed and recycled, allowing their metals to be put to good further use.

On a larger scale, the reclamation of metals such as iron and steel is vital, both to the economy of our own nation and to the world as a whole. It is a major industry in its own right, yet one in which we can all participate. In the UK the British Scrap Federation coordinates the work of scrap metal merchants and processors who supply the scrap metal requirements of the steel industry.

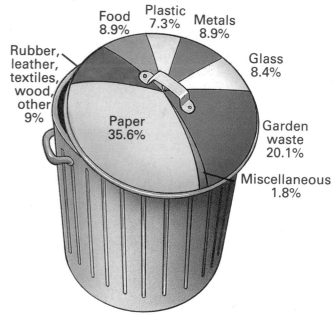

Metals make up 9 per cent of household waste. (Figures from US Environmental Protection Agency.)

Household metal – junk or valued? This skip contains a wide range of items discarded from the home that are a valuable source of metal scrap.

We live in a throwaway age and it is all too easy to dispose of scrap metal in a thoughtless way. Small items are frequently tossed into the dustbin when they could well be sorted and reclaimed for scrap. Larger items are even more problematic. This car has been abandoned. Not only would it have value as scrap metal. It is also spoiling the beauty of the landscape.

Recycling begins at home. From time to time every household considers how to dispose of unwanted items such as an old refrigerator, washing machine or bicycle, all of which are valuable for recycling back into the metal industry.

Recycling enables vital supplies of the world's raw materials to be saved. It also reduces the need to transport materials to processing plants. Metal recycling saves energy too: making steel from scrap uses approximately one quarter of the energy needed to convert raw iron ore into steel; recycling aluminium uses only 5 per cent of the energy required to make aluminium from bauxite. Anyone interested in conservation and the quality of our environment will appreciate such advantages associated with the use of recycled scrap metal. Recycling causes far less pollution of the air, water and soil, and it does not use the large amounts of water which are required when steel is produced from raw materials.

All of these ideas are elaborated upon in the forthcoming pages, but at this stage one key fact should be emphasized: a much larger proportion of the world's waste must be recycled, a task which should be of concern to every individual. Recycling begins at

home, and without doubt WASTE METAL = WEALTH. The remainder of this book takes a more detailed look at certain metals, their uses and possibilities for recycling. It outlines case studies of good practice and, more importantly, suggests ways in which more people may become involved in this action.

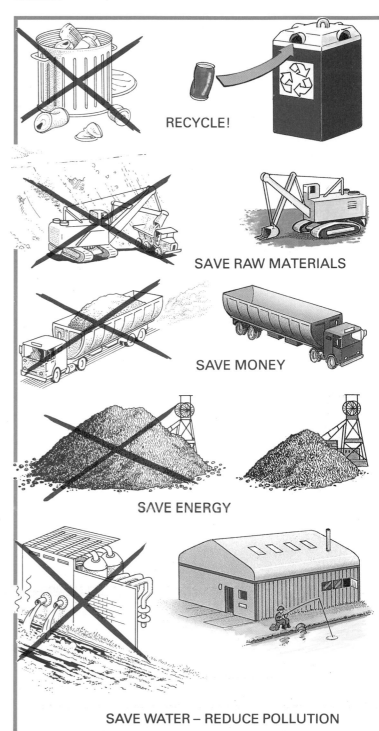

RECYCLE!

SAVE RAW MATERIALS

SAVE MONEY

SAVE ENERGY

SAVE WATER – REDUCE POLLUTION

THE IRON AND STEEL INDUSTRY

This blast furnace is for making iron. It is situated at Redcar, Teesside, and is the largest in Europe. It is operated by British Steel.

Iron is the world's most used metal. A mineral called iron ore, together with coal and limestone are the three key raw materials needed for making it. In turn, iron can be transformed into steel.

A large construction known as a blast furnace is used for making iron. Within this huge oven, coals are heated for many hours. The raw materials of coke (coals), ore and limestone are fed in through the top of the furnace. At the same time, air, heated to an extremely high temperature, is forced under high pressure into part of the furnace known as the melting zone. The hot air enables the coke to burn fiercely, so that great heat and a large amount of gas are produced. This is carried upwards to an outlet near the top of the furnace. The gas reacts with the ore and other raw materials to produce a substance called metallic iron, which melts and is carried down to the bottom of the furnace. Whilst this is happening, the limestone mixes with impurities in the ore and coke to form molten slag which settles on top of the iron. This process continues uninterrupted and the slag and metallic iron are "run off", or removed separately, through outlets in the base of the furnace. The metallic iron can then be transferred elsewhere to be made into steel. Most of the impurities in the iron (for example, silicon, sulphur, phosphorus) are removed and the amount of carbon it contains is reduced.

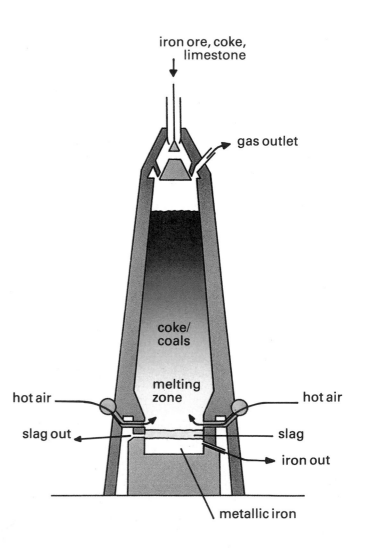

The workings of a blast furnace.

The iron may be dealt with in a number of ways, perhaps in a Basic Oxygen Converter. This device can tilt forwards and backwards. First, some scrap steel is put into it, followed by the molten iron. A long tube then pipes oxygen into the converter and on to the surface of the iron. This results in a chemical change so that impurities are removed and the iron is transformed into molten steel. The molten steel is poured out of the converter into special moulds where it cools and becomes solid, creating blocks of metal known as steel ingots.

The ingots may be heated, rolled into thinner strips and cut into lengths called slabs. These are then cooled and inspected before being heated once again. The reheated metal enters a hot strip-mill, where it is reduced in thickness until it becomes a coil of thin steel or sheet that can be sold to industrial customers.

This whole process is dependent on the mineral iron ore. Like all other minerals found on our earth, iron ore is a finite, non-renewable resource – in other words, if we use it all up it is gone for ever. Known reserves, from which iron may be extracted, are unevenly distributed in the crust of the earth. It is difficult to predict the consumption of minerals and to estimate how long reserves will last. At the time of writing iron is in good supply, yet some scientists are pessimistic. In the USA good-quality iron deposits in the states of Minnesota and Michigan have been badly depleted and the proportion of imported ore is increasing. It has been estimated that the life expectancy of iron ore may be only 100 – 200 years. Without doubt, efforts must be made to conserve resources: one major way to achieve this is through successful recycling of iron and steel.

A basic oxygen converter. Molten steel can be poured out of the converter into moulds.

Steelmaking takes place in a similar way throughout the world. This blast furnace is transforming iron into steel in Argentina.

ANY OLD IRON AND STEEL?

Reclamation of iron and steel is vital for the conservation of earth's finite resources and to the economy of individual nations and the world as a whole. It is a major industry in its own right. In the UK the British Scrap Federation coordinates the work of some 600 scrap merchants and processors, who share the task of supplying the scrap requirements of the steel industry.

Waste material for reclamation and recycling comes from three main sources. First, there are large scrap-producing industries from which regular collections are made. Second, much is derived from the demolition and dismantling of buildings and equipment constructed from metal. Third, there are thousands of "small" collectors of metal, many of whom travel around our neighbourhoods crying out "Any old iron and steel?" whilst collecting discarded tools, broken washing machines, battered bicycles and any other junk metal. These collectors may then sell their junk to larger scrap processors.

The UK scrap metal industry probably ranks as one of the best equipped and most efficient and competitive in the world. More capital investment has gone into it in recent years than into almost any other industry. All scrap collected is sorted, graded and processed before being delivered in bulk to steelmakers and foundries for recycling.

It costs around £1,000,000 to set up a medium-sized scrap-processing plant. In 1919, when the national Scrap Federation was established, hammers, hacksaws and chisels were the tools used for breaking up metal; strong men with shovels and forks, aided by horses and carts, would move it about. Today, a well-equipped processing plant contains "hydraulic shears", "fragmenters" and "balers" which break, cut, shred and then bale the metal for its return to the steel industry. It must be stressed that not only iron, but large amounts of non-ferrous scrap (i.e. not containing iron) are recovered at the same time. Many processing plants have departments dealing with non-ferrous metals such as copper, lead and brass, since these are also valuable materials for recycling.

Scrap metal derives from three sources. These are the large scrap-producing industries, the dismantling of buildings, and the "small", itinerant collectors of junk metal.

All scrap is sorted, graded and processed before being delivered to the steel industry. This scrap has passed through the first stages of recovery and is waiting for shredding and cutting.

After it has been broken up and shredded, the metal is then baled so that it can be returned to the steelmakers for re-use.

Scrap processing is a vital industry for economic and environmental reasons. At present, almost 60 per cent of the steel in Britain and virtually all the cast iron and refined iron are made from scrap metal. Without this, we would have to spend hundreds of millions of pounds on importing additional raw materials. Recycling metal saves energy, conserves water and finite mineral reserves and reduces air pollution. Worldwide, the heavy steel industry uses scrap for some 50 per cent of its iron requirements. The USA is the world's leading nation in the scrap business, where 35 per cent of heavy metals are recycled. Most of this material comes from used machinery, transport and construction materials. In 1989 the US exported around 11 million tonnes of iron and steel scrap. However, in many nations and indeed globally, there is much room for improvement in recycling efforts.

At this shredding plant the disintegrated and sorted metal awaits baling. Today these processes are carried out with the aid of modern machinery – a far cry from the early days of reclamation when men used hacksaws and chisels for the task!

FOOD CANS: THE GOOD, THE BAD AND THE UGLY

Over 11,000,000,000 cans are purchased in Britain every year – and that figure is constantly rising! Worldwide, most cans are made from either tinplate or aluminium, or a combination of the two metals. Tinplate is a sheet of high-quality steel coated with very fine layers of pure tin. The tin protects the can from corrosion.

Food cans have been around for almost 200 years. In 1795 Napoleon offered a prize to anyone who could find a method of preserving food for the soldiers in his armies. The prize was won in 1810 by a Frenchman who did interesting work in sterilizing food. In the same year, an Englishman named Peter Durand designed a tin-plated iron can that would act as a food container. All of these early cans were made of iron and coated with a thin layer of tin. Manufacturers could make 60 of them in a day.

Since then, numerous developments and inventions have revolutionized the canning industry. In 1890, the first automatic can-making machinery was introduced in the UK. In 1935, beer came in cans for the first time. 1963 saw the invention of the ring-pull aluminium can, and in 1964 manufacturers in the USA developed a can made only of two pieces of aluminium. The first tin-free steel cans were made in Britain in 1968. Modern can-making factories produce over 1,000,000 cans a day compared to the 60 of 1810!

Canned foods are extremely convenient. With a store of canned foods in your cupboard, you can produce a meal easily, even if the shops are shut. Canned foods have already been prepared and cooked, and so need only to be reheated before serving: this saves time and effort. Canned food is

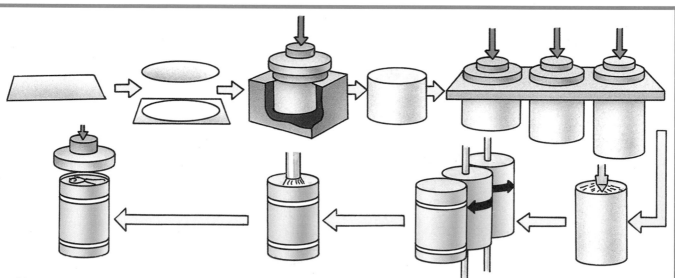

How a two-piece drink can is made. A circle is stamped out of an aluminium sheet and then pressed into a mould to make a cylindrical container about half the height that the can will be when it is finished. This container is further pressed, or stamped, so that the sides become thinner and taller, but the base remains thicker. The inside of the can is sprayed, to prevent the contents from being contaminated, and the outside is printed. The can is filled with drink and an aluminium ring-pull lid is sealed on top.

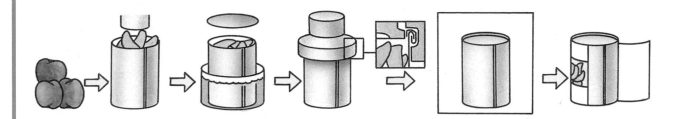

Canning. Fresh food is cleaned, prepared and blanched and put into sterile cans, together with some liquid. The cans are heated in hot water, to remove air, and then sealed. Next the cans are heated in a steam-pressure container, to make the contents sterile, and finally the labels are added.

good quality because only first-class foods are selected for canning and no artificial preservatives are added: it is the actual cooking and canning process which preserves the food. Food in cans lasts a long time if kept in a cool, dry place. It does not need to take up space in a refrigerator. Similar advantages could be listed for canned drinks.

Unfortunately, the value of cans is offset by some bad and ugly aspects of their use. Cans and ring-pulls are tossed aside as litter, spoiling our environment and creating hazardous waste. Many birds and animals die each year, cut by the rough edges of broken cans or by swallowing ring-pulls.

The answer, of course, is recycling. An aluminium can thrown out of a car window could still be littering the earth in 500 years' time. One aluminium can recycled saves energy equivalent to that needed to operate your television set for three hours.

All of the general economic and ecological arguments put forward in favour of heavy metal recycling obviously hold true for cans, which, indeed, form part of the scrap metal industry. Can recycling helps to preserve the earth's finite resources. It saves money, energy and materials, and reduces the volume of solid waste. Furthermore, it helps to prevent our world being spoilt by hazardous and unsightly litter.

Two-piece drink cans leaving a can-making line.

ALUMINIUM: PROBLEMS AND RECYCLING

Aluminium is the second most used metal after iron. It is actually the most abundant metal on earth, but is only possible to extract in certain areas. It was discovered as recently as the 1820s, and is one of the most expensive and polluting metals to produce. It is extracted from bauxite ore, which is found in abundance in tropical forest areas. Most of the aluminium used in the United States, for example, is imported from Guinea, Australia and Brazil. Scientists predict that the apparently plentiful supplies of bauxite will run out in 50 – 100 years.

Open-cast bauxite mining in tropical forests causes major concern to environmentalists. The process destroys natural vegetation, leaving soil bare and subject to erosion. Tropical insects, birds and mammals lose their habitats, with far-reaching effects on the numbers and diversity of living things in the area. To make the problem worse, much slag is left behind where bauxite is extracted. Since a series of chemical processes is necessary to produce the actual aluminium metal, many pollutants are released into the atmosphere, including fluorine gas.

Some people might argue that aluminium cans should never be produced, when obtaining the raw material for them can cause so much environmental and ecological damage. One certain fact is that aluminium can recycling is essential and should be promoted throughout the world; indeed, ALL aluminium should be recycled, including kitchen foil, pie-plates, frozen food trays and building materials. The largest single use of the metal, however, is

for the beverage can. In the United States in 1989 more than 75 thousand million beverage cans were used, of which 95 per cent were aluminium. Another staggering statistic is that making aluminium from recycled aluminium uses 90 per cent less energy than making it from raw materials.

It is estimated that worldwide, 80 per cent of all aluminium cans could be recycled. In fact, only 30 per cent of world production is derived from scrap. In the United States, half of the aluminium cans sold are now recovered and recycled; the UK figure is considerably lower. However, the can-making industry, other organizations, local authorities and individuals are doing much to promote and develop recycling schemes. Various drinks-can manufacturers have organized collaborative efforts to promote recycling of all kinds of metal cans (see pages 20-21). Some schemes, however, are specially designed to promote the recycling of aluminium. You can distinguish aluminium cans from others because they are not magnetic (check this by using magnets found on refrigerator or cupboard doors).

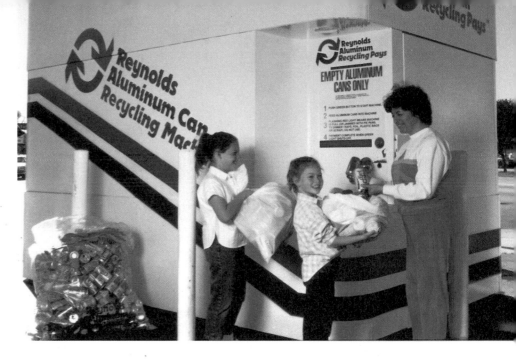

A bauxite mine in the Northern Territory of Australia.

Can banks are growing in popularity throughout the world. The Reynolds Aluminium Recycling Company in the United States purchases used cans from the public. New aluminium drink cans can be made from 100 per cent recycled metal.

The number of aluminium cans recycled in the United States

1970: 6 cans per person

1987: 157 cans per person

Recycling is "on the up". In the United States there has been a major upsurge of interest in recycling since 1970. This trend is occurring throughout the world.

In 1987 the aluminium industry set up a recycling scheme in Birmingham, and in the first eighteen months, 150 tonnes of the metal were collected in the city. This initiative expanded into the Aluminium Can Recycling Association, which operates nationwide. Since aluminium has a high scrap value, collecting cans for recycling is a good way to raise money for charity. Recycled aluminium is passed into a secondary smelting process where it is melted down for re-use by the aluminium industry.

The message is very clear. Every can recycled helps to conserve raw materials, saves energy and protects the environment of the world's tropical forests.

At this ALCAN van, aluminium cans are "bought back" from the consumer for recycling.

STEEL CANS: TIN AND BI-METAL RECYCLING

Tin cans are made of steel, with a thin coating of tin to prevent corrosion of the steel. Bi-metal cans (more common in the USA) are tin-coated steel with one or both ends made of aluminium. Many drinks cans are tin-plated steel with an aluminium top and ring-pull. Recycling these cans is much more difficult than recycling all-aluminium ones.

950 million steel cans are recycled in the UK each year. This total includes drinks cans (around 150 million), as well as food, petfood and aerosol cans. Whilst much emphasis is put on encouraging the public to recycle drinks cans, these actually form only a small part of the steel recycling potential.

Steel cans are reclaimed for recycling in two ways. They can be collected by means of "Save-a-Can" schemes, in which people take their used cans to a special skip. There were only around 180 "Save-a-Can" collection points in England and Wales in 1990, compared with 4,000 bottle banks. Otherwise, steel cans can be separated from household waste after it has been collected by the local authority. As collected waste travels along a conveyor belt, large electromagnets attract and separate the steel. Only 22 local authorities (7 per cent) extract steel from waste in this way. If more did so, this would save on the cost of organizing and publicizing voluntary collection schemes.

Save-a-Can schemes are an important element of recycling initiatives in the UK. Consumers are encouraged to take along used steel cans and deposit them in a skip. The number of Save-a-Can sites is increasing.

Food cans, petfood cans, aerosol cans – any family's regular shopping trip to the supermarket will probably result in a wide variety of cans being purchased.

Used steel cans are collected at waste processing plants using a magnetized conveyor belt.

Thousands of steel cans can be collected at waste disposal incinerators by means of large electromagnets and used to make new steel products.

Sometimes steel cans are removed before the rest of the waste is incinerated. Sometimes the metal is extracted after incineration. In the latter case, the metal is returned to British Steel for re-use. Cans extracted from waste that has not been incinerated are processed to remove any tin and leave very good-quality scrap steel. Incinerated cans do not need this de-tinning treatment before they can be remelted in the steelworks, but cannot be recycled into a high-quality product.

Steel from cans forms only a tiny part of the total steel scrap derived from industrial nations, but its potential must not be underestimated. Every contribution at a local level forms part of a partnership between individuals and industry that will have some impact on global metal conservation.

19

THE CAN-MAKERS: COOPERATION FOR RECYCLING

If any substantial progress is to be made in recycling, then partnership and cooperation are essential. The Can-Makers organization of the United Kingdom, formed in 1981, is dedicated to conserving energy and preserving raw materials. It represents the five large United Kingdom producers of beer and soft drinks cans, namely American Can, Continental Can, Crown Cork, Metal Box and Nacanco, plus their suppliers of aluminium and tinplate.

The Can-Makers body works closely with the Metal Packaging Manufacturers Association to promote good management of resources and recycling of metals. Recent attention to the quantity of resources used has led to a dramatic reduction in the materials needed for making cans. Can walls are now made thinner, in a process known as lightweighting. In 1970 a typical fizzy drinks can weighed 57g; it now weighs 35g. For the millions of cans that are made, this change means a huge saving in metal. Similarly, making steel ready for can-making now takes 25 per cent less energy than it did a decade ago. Also, brewers and fizzy drinks manufacturers have found ways of conserving energy on their can-filling conveyors. Can shapes have been altered to conserve metal. Reducing the diameter of a can at the end (known as "necking in") saves materials. As with thickness, a tiny saving of material in making one can adds up to a huge saving of materials worldwide. Finally, in the can-making process, when parts of a can are stamped out of a coil of metal, all the scrap is now recycled by the industry. All these developments make economic sense and represent a great conservation achievement.

Lightweighting

1970

57g

1990

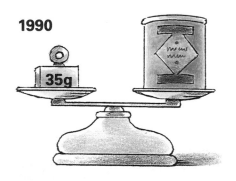

35g

Cans are now made with much thinner walls. This considerably reduces the amount of metal required for their manufacture.

The AMG waste metal processing plant is at Hartlepool in Cleveland. Here tin is removed, leaving good-quality scrap steel for re-use.

The Can-Makers fund the recycling of all types of can through the "Save-a-Can" scheme, which began in 1980. Skips are loaned free of charge to local authorities, who are asked to place them where large numbers of the public are likely to pass by – the car park of a supermarket is an obvious choice. People are asked to save all kinds of cans and deposit them in the skips. For every tonne of metal collected, the Can-Makers organization makes a donation to a charity chosen by the local authority. "Save-a-Can" pays for haulage and transport, including taking the cans to a de-tinning plant at Hartlepool in the north-east of England. Here, aluminium and tinplate cans are separated. Aluminium cans are sent on to aluminium secondary smelters and the others are de-tinned at Hartlepool.

Saving a can aids charity and conserves raw materials.

Producing three-piece cans at AHI Metal Containers in Aukland, New Zealand.

WHERE THE ACTION IS: THEY RECYCLE

Throughout Europe, metal collection points and removal services are common. In Switzerland, there are special collection bins for aluminium, and trial bins for food tins. The town of Freiburg has recently introduced a system of rubbish containers for all useful materials. These are known as "green bins" and householders are asked to deposit all recyclable items which are then collected and sorted. Of the waste collected in 1989, 8 per cent was scrap metal.

In a "cash for cans" scheme the idea is that people pay a deposit added to the price of every can purchased; and this deposit is returned to them when they take the can back for recycling. The UK Can-Makers believe this would be ineffective and expensive to operate: the costs would be passed on directly to the consumer, through rising prices of canned food and drink. However, a "cash for cans" scheme works well in Sweden, where more cans are made of aluminium, which has a higher scrap value than steel.

A European Economic Community directive on liquid containers specifies that there shall be no legislation to impose a deposit system, and suggests that voluntary programmes are

Examples of Deposit Laws in some US States

STATE	EFFECTIVE DATE	
Connecticut	January, 1980	Minimum $.05 deposit Container handling fee: soft drink=$.02; beer=$.01 Bans sale of detachable pull-tabs on beverage containers
Delaware	July, 1982	Minimum $.05 deposit Minimum 20 percent handling fee Bans detachable pull-tabs on beverage containers Provides for the establishment of redemption centers
Maine	January, 1979	Minimum $.05 deposit Minimum $.02 handling fee Bans detachable pull-tabs on beverage containers Bans nonbiodegradable plastic containers
New York	September, 1983	Minimum $.05 deposit Minimum one-and-a-half cent handling fee Bans detachable pull-tabs on beverage containers Bans plastic secondary packaging that is not photodegradable or biodegradable Provides for the establishment of redemption centers Requires that bottlers pick up empty containers from retailers and pay handling fee within the same credit arrangement as the sale of full goods Requires bottlers to report amount of unclaimed deposits to the state as the Commissioner deems necessary
Vermont	January, 1975	Minimum $.05 deposit Minimum 40 percent handling fee Bans detachable pull-tabs on beverage containers Provides for the establishment of redemption centers Bans plastic or nonbiodegradable "connecting devices"

Individuals have a key role to play in recycling. This young citizen has collected and sorted cans as well as bottles, ready for kerbside collection in a community programme established in Ohio, USA.

Recycling often means innovation. In Kenya, oil lamps have been made out of old cans.

more desirable and effective. Deposit legislation is a part of life for some consumers in the United States. The state of Oregon, for example, passed a bottle bill in 1972, putting a deposit on beverage cans. Shortly after this, Oregon's litter increased by 12 per cent and consumers had to pay around 22 per cent more for their drinks, not including the returnable deposit. This evidence, together with a report in the state of New York, supports the view that deposit legislation is not effective.

Most American states have approached recycling by seeking voluntary contributions. Results have been excellent: Americans are recycling more aluminium cans than ever before and, as in Britain, the schemes include giving donations to charity and so millions of dollars have been received by worthwhile organizations. Many US recycling schemes are based on a mixture of methods, including door-to-door collections, collection points and mechanical extraction from waste.

The city of San Jose, California, is but one example of success in the USA. The largest and most sophisticated multi-material processing centre in central California was recently opened there. Residents place recyclable materials in special containers provided by the city at the side of the street in a "kerbside programme". These bins are regularly emptied and the contents delivered to the processing plant for weighing and sorting. Metal cans (separated from paper and glass) are conveyed to a sorting station where contaminants are removed, then a magnet separates the steel from the aluminium. The average participating household recycles some 600 pounds (272 kg) of solid waste a year, including 15 lb (6.8kg) of tin and 7 lb (3.2kg) of aluminium. The director of the San Jose Office of Environmental Management says that: "The kerbside recycling programme is an integral part of the City Council's adopted solid waste strategy. It will be the single most important factor in helping the city keep garbage rates affordable in the long run."

WHERE THE ACTION CAN BE: YOU RECYCLE

The success of large-scale ventures like the San Jose kerbside programme and the Aluminium Can Recycling Association still depends on individual commitment. Each and every one of us can take action. Recycling begins at home. Look out for "Save-a-Can" skips. Contact your local authority and ask if your area has a recycling scheme. If not, encourage people to do something about starting one.

Recycling cans takes very little time and effort. There are two simple rules for preparing used cans: rinse them out when you have finished washing up (use the washing-up water to conserve fresh tap supplies!) and then squash them. Squashed cans take up far less space, both for you to store them before taking them for recycling and within the skip itself. The more cans fitted into the skip, the more money will be raised for charity. An added advantage is that your dustbin without the cans will have much more room for other waste.

Preparing cans for recycling is important but not very time-consuming. They should be rinsed out in used washing-up water (don't waste fresh tap water), and then squashed flat.

One can will have a lonely journey – and will cost a lot of petrol money to deliver!

At this collection point in Hampshire, consumers are encouraged to "feed the green machine" with used aluminium cans.

Make sure that you deposit your cans safely inside the skip. Money is paid for those IN the skip, not for those on the ground. Guard against litter at all costs. If the skip is full, the only sensible action is to be patient and bring your cans back another day.

As well as personally delivering cans, enquire about door-to-door collections. If these are not organized by the local authority, charities and other organizations may be prepared to collect used metal goods from you. Keep aluminium cans separate from steel ones (use a magnet to tell them apart), as aluminium scrap fetches a higher price than steel.

Metal cans are likely to remain a feature of our lives. The Can-Makers commissioned a research study into attitudes to the packaging of drinks. It showed that cans are associated with good quality and good flavour; they are thought to be better insulators than plastic and cartons, thus keeping their contents cool for a longer time. The can's image also seems important: according to the Can-Makers' study, young people think it looks trendy to be seen with a can, and men certainly claim to enjoy their beer at home from cans. Finally, consumers emphasized the convenience of cans. Hopefully, such enthusiasm for canned goods will continue into enthusiasm for dealing thoughtfully with the empty cans.

Remember that metal recycling goes beyond the drinks can. Look for opportunities to recycle other aluminium goods (for instance, foil, trays, food containers) and never thoughtlessly dispose of household goods that are made of valuable and recyclable metals. Your local authority will always advise on the collection of "any old iron and steel".

CONCLUSIONS

Individual action plus industrial commitment is a powerful force in the development of worthwhile recycling programmes, but action must go hand in hand with information, development and research. Research and development are constantly being undertaken in the metal industry. Recent steps forward in technology have opened up new options for more economic recycling of steel. New techniques allow better use of natural resources, decrease energy consumption and reduce waste. Throughout the world, the industry is committed to good resource management, taking account of both costs and ecological principles.

Such major developments in large industries may seem very remote from individual people and everyday life. But we all need to receive basic information about waste management and recycling so that we understand the need for action and how to get involved. The various organizations and resources listed on page 28 will provide further information about recycling in general or of metals in particular. Also consult your local authority and ask in the community. Here are some useful questions to ask:

★ How is solid waste collection/management organized?
★ Who is responsible for the management of waste?
★ What is the local budget for solid waste management?
★ What is the composition of waste in your neighbourhood?

Remember, individual action is an essential part of the world's recycling initiatives. These young citizens set the example.

Recycling can indeed be innovative as well as a responsibility. These children in the Sudan are enjoying toy cars that have been made out of metal scrap collected locally.

★ How much of the waste is placed in landfills?
★ Where is the landfill that your community's waste goes to?
★ Does your community have an incinerator?
★ Does your community have a recycling programme?
★ Are there door-to-door collections?
★ Where are the collection points?

You could even start a recycling scheme yourself. The Aluminium Can Recycling Association will give all the advice you need. Persuade friends and neighbours to help. If you contact ALUCAN, they will register you as an official collector, send collecting bags and provide further information.

As well as taking individual action towards recycling, we can all encourage our local communities to adopt recycling measures and to consider large-scale schemes. Underpinning all of this are the essential reasons for reducing waste as a whole:

★ To extend the earth's energy resources
★ To extend the earth's mineral resources
★ To reduce the pollution associated with industry and energy use
★ To reduce environmental/ecological problems related to the disposal of waste

With combined understanding and action from industry and individuals, a great deal can be achieved in terms of making metal a beneficial rather than a problematic part of our world.

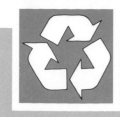

GLOSSARY

blast furnace large furnace in which iron is extracted from raw materials

corrosion wearing away by chemical action

ferrous containing iron

finite resources resources available in a limited supply, for example, coal and oil. One day we may use them all up

impurities "foreign" matter, causing a substance not to be pure

pollute to make dirty, foul or unclean

recycling the conversion of waste into a reusable product

waste that which is left over after use, superfluous, no longer serving a purpose

ADDRESSES

Aluminium Can Recycling Association
1 Mex House, 52 Blucher Street,
Birmingham B1 1QV

British Scrap Federation, 16 High Street,
Brompton, Huntingdon,
Cambridgeshire PE18 8TU

BSC Tin Plate, P.O. Box 101, Velindre,
Swansea, West Glamorgan SA5 5WW

Can-Makers Information Service
36 Grosvenor Gardens, London SW1W OED

Community Recycling Opportunities Programme
7 Burner's Lane, Kiln Farm,
Milton Keynes MK11 3HA

Friends of the Earth, 26/28 Underwood Street,
London N1 7JQ

Tidy Britain Group, publications available from
The Pier, Wigan, WN3 4EX

Waste Watch, 26 Bedford Square,
London WC1B 3HU

RESOURCES

For further reading and information (send a stamped, addressed envelope for details of costs).

1) *Waste Issues* information pack from the Tidy Britain Group

2) Factsheets and Information Packs from the Can-Makers Information Service

3) Information Sheets from "Save-a-Can"

4) Useful literature from the British Scrap Federation

5) Steel Can Recycling Progress leaflet from BSC Tin Plate

6) Teacher's File, from Aluminium Can Recycling Association

7) The Dustbin Pack, teacher's file, from Waste Watch

8) *Recycling* poster, available from Pictorial Charts Educational Trust, 27 Kirchen Road, London W13 OUD

In Australia, further information can be obtained from the following agencies in each capital city:

Environmental Protection Agency
Keep Australia Beautiful
Total Environment Centre
Waste Management Authority
or Your Local Council

INDEX

PRINTED IN BELGIUM BY
proost
INTERNATIONAL BOOK PRODUCTION